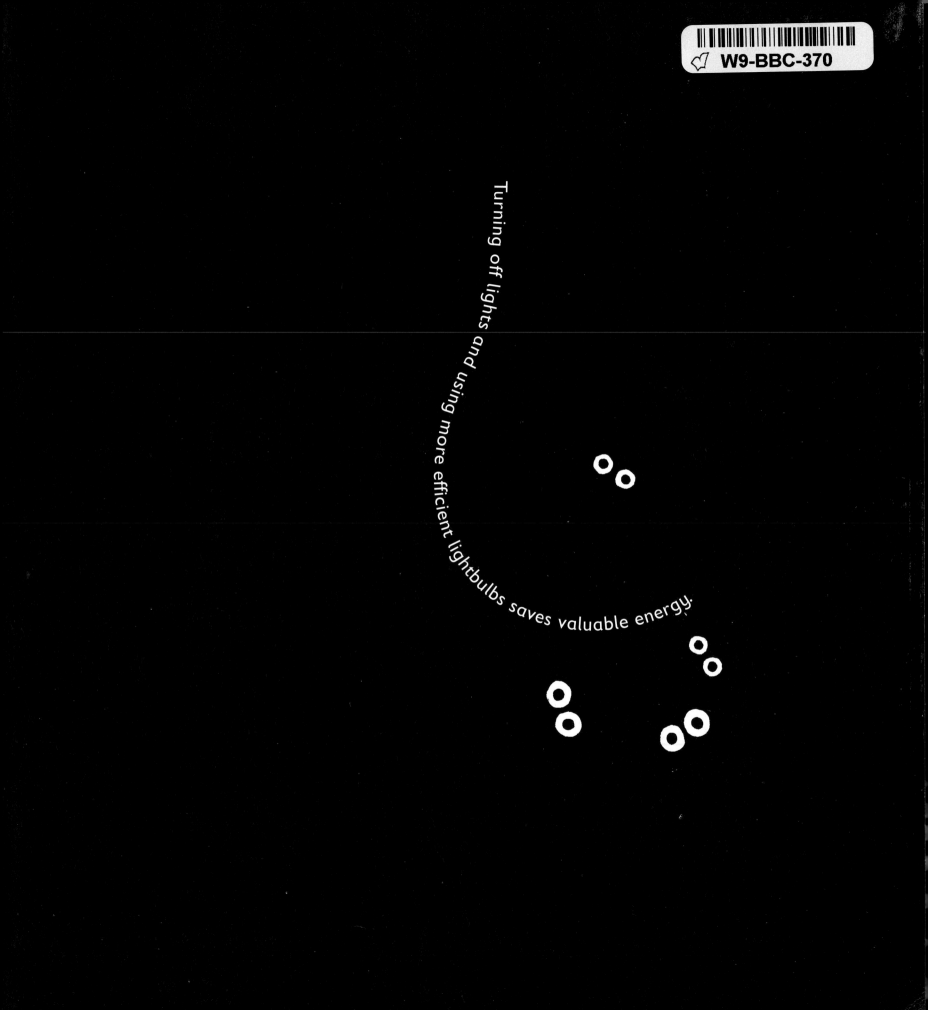

Turning off lights and using more efficient lightbulbs saves valuable energy.

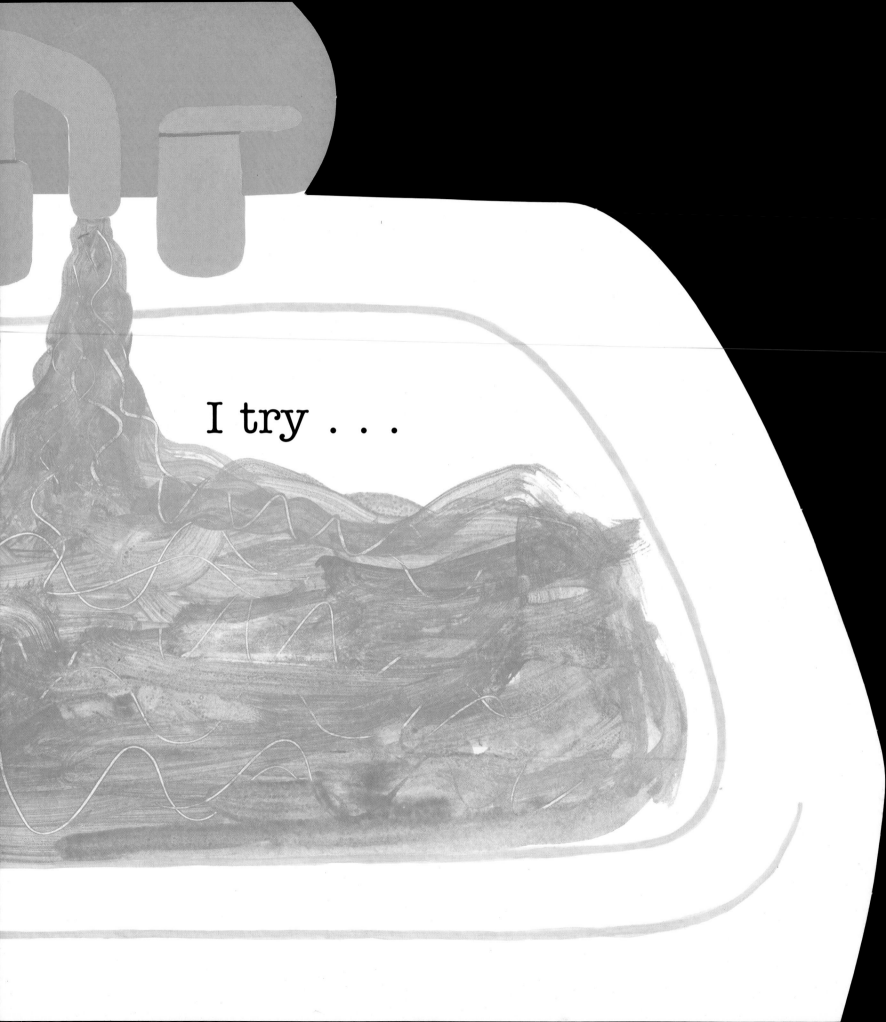

I try . . .

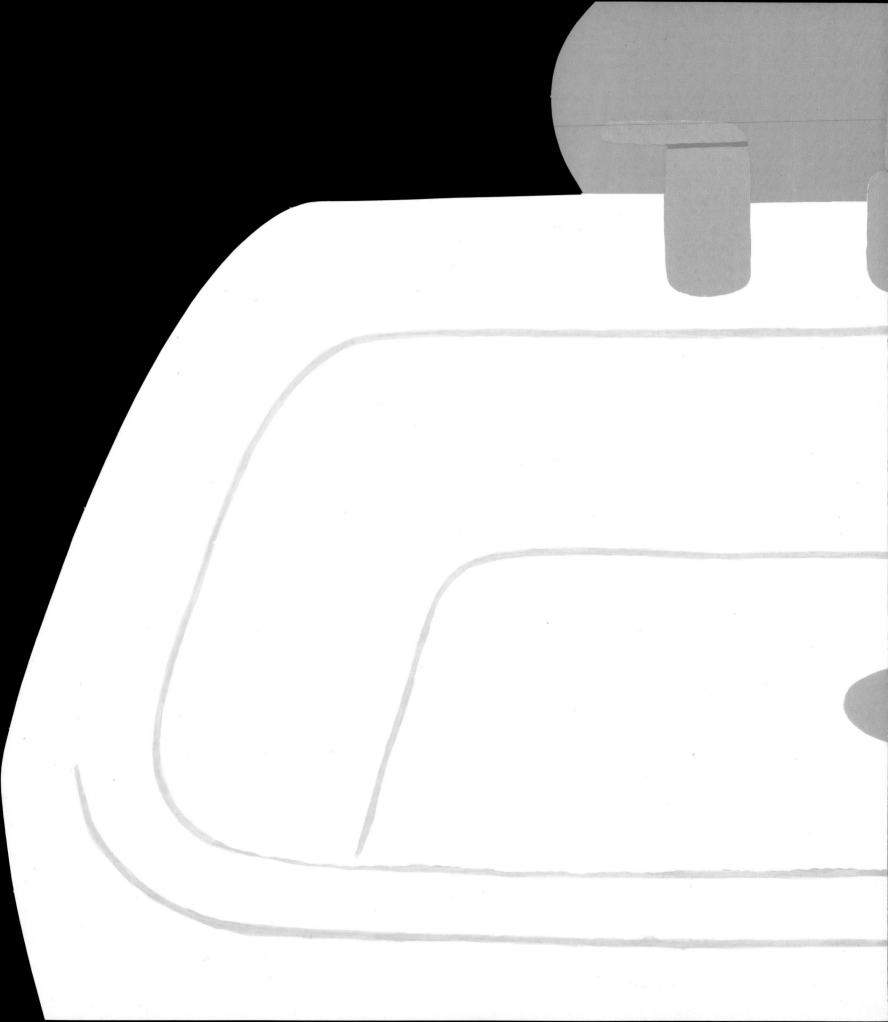

to turn off
the tap when I
brush my teeth.

Every time you do this, you save eighteen glasses of water.

I always . . .

TRASH

Putting garbage away keeps the world safe and clean.

I will . . .

feed the
birds in winter.

Feeding the birds helps them get ready for nesting in the spring.

I use . . .

If everybody did this, it would greatly reduce the number of trees we use to make paper.

both sides of the paper.

I remind
my parents . . .

I enjoy . . .

making toys from things
around the house.

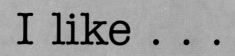

I like . . .

to walk to school.

Avoiding car trips saves gas and cuts down on air pollution. Walking is also good exercise.

I can . . .

Plants help keep the air clean and healthy.

I help . . .

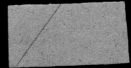